NOTORIOUS AMERICANS AND THEIR TIMES

Benedict

ARNOLD

and the American Revolution

by

DAVID C. KING

Consulting Editor

GREGORY H. NOBLES
Georgia Institute of Technology

BLACKBIRCH PRESS, INC.

WOODBRIDGE, CONNECTICUT

Published by Blackbirch Press, Inc.
260 Amity Road
Woodbridge, CT 06525

e-mail: staff@blackbirch.com
Web site: www.blackbirch.com

©1999 by Blackbirch Press, Inc.
First Edition

Printed in the United States

10 9 8 7 6 5 4 3

Library of Congress Cataloging-in-Publication Data
King, David C.
Benedict Arnold and the American Revolution / by David C. King.
    p.   cm. — (Notorious Americans and their times)
    Includes bibliographical references and index.
    Summary: Examines the life of the brilliant general who became America's most infamous Revolutionary War traitor.
    ISBN 1-56711-221-8 (lib. bdg. : alk. paper)
    1. Arnold, Benedict, 1741–1801—Juvenile literature. 2. American loyalists—United States—Biography—Juvenile literature. 3. Generals—United States—Biography—Juvenile literature. 4. United States—Continental Army—Biography—Juvenile literature. 5. United States—History—Revolution, 1775–1783—Biography—Juvenile literature.
[1. Arnold, Benedict, 1741–1801. 2. American loyalists. 3. Generals.
4. United States—History—Revolution, 1775–1783—Biography.]
I. Title. II. Series.
E278.A7K56   1999
973.3'82'092—dc21   98-11580
[B]   CIP
                                        AC

Table of Contents

Chapter 1

THE PATH TO WAR
A SON OF LIBERTY

*A*n unusual military monument sits on the grounds of Saratoga National Historical Park, overlooking the Hudson River, in New York State. A sculpture of an American Revolutionary War officer's boot carries this inscription:

In memory of the most brilliant soldier in the Continental Army, who was desperately wounded on this spot, 7th October, 1777, winning for his countrymen the decisive battle of the American Revolution.

There is no name on the monument. This is how Americans chose to honor the most heroic action in the military career of Benedict Arnold.

Opposite: *Additional British troops entered Boston in 1774 after the Boston Tea Party.*

How did "the most brilliant soldier," become so despised by his country that his name was left off of a monument to his heroism? By understanding Arnold's troubled but fascinating life, the reader will gain a better understanding of America's struggle for independence and creation of a new nation.

Arnold Learns a Trade

As a soldier, Benedict Arnold was known for his extraordinary courage. Yet he once confided to a friend, "I was a coward until I was fifteen." A change in the family's fortunes may explain why the youthful Benedict suddenly decided to show the world how brave he could be.

From the time of his birth in Norwich Town, Connecticut, on January 14, 1741, Benedict Arnold's path in life seemed secure. He was the only son of a wealthy merchant. On Sundays, Benedict, his younger sister, Hannah, and their parents sat in the first row of pews in church. The Arnolds' private pews were symbols of their important position in society.

While any young man with unusual energy and some luck could rise in Colonial society, the sons of leading families had significant advantages. A son of a wealthy family was sent to private schools—unlike his sisters, who were educated at home. If he chose to, a young man could continue his education at one of several Colonial colleges. Then he might work in his family's business or become a doctor, lawyer, or church minister. He might even play a role in Colonial government.

Benedict Arnold expected to follow this traditional path to success. It was suddenly closed off to him, though, when his father's trading business failed, and the family's wealth disappeared. His father became a helpless alcoholic and the object of town gossip and cruel jokes. In response to the family's shame,

Arnold, then 15 years old, began engaging in wild acts of daring. He once walked along the roof of a barn that had caught on fire. On another occasion, he tipped over a cannon on the village green, stuffed the barrel with gunpowder, and ignited it, causing a terrific explosion that could have killed him.

When the family could no longer afford to send Benedict to private school, his mother signed him on as an apprentice to Dr. Daniel Lathrop, the owner of a busy apothecary shop (drugstore). Lathrop was a relative of the Arnolds. As an apprentice, Benedict worked for him without pay and in exchange learned an apothecary's trade. It was a good position for him. While working for Lathrop from the ages of 15 to 21, Arnold learned more than how to prepare and sell medicines. He also learned about importing luxury goods, such as silks, perfume, wines, and works of art. Arnold liked the luxury of the Lathrops' lovely mansion, where he enjoyed fine foods and the comfort of being waited on by the family's slaves.

A Struggle for Empire

While Arnold was an apprentice, war broke out between Great Britain and France. The Seven Years' War (1754–1763) was a struggle between the world's two most powerful nations, who wanted to expand their empires throughout the world. In North America (where the struggle became known as the French and Indian War) the French fought the British from their sprawling, sparsely populated colony of New France (now Canada). With the help of some Native American tribes, the French set out to conquer Britain's 13 American colonies.

In 1757, a French invasion force moved south into the colony of New York and established a fort at the southern end of Lake Champlain. Benedict Arnold, then 16, received permission from the Lathrops to join the Connecticut militia. The militia marched toward Lake Champlain, but the battle ended before Arnold's company arrived.

After two years of disastrous defeats for the British and the Colonial militia, their luck improved dramatically. The British won on all fronts and, in the peace treaty of 1763, Canada became part of the British Empire. The American colonists joined in celebrating Britain's great triumph and erected statues to honor young King George III, who had become king in 1760.

Open for Business

After Arnold completed his apprenticeship in 1762, the Lathrops gave him enough money to start his own business. He moved to New Haven, Connecticut, and opened his own apothecary shop. Running the shop gave him a chance to travel to London

An accounting room at an eighteenth-century business.

to order luxury goods and outfit himself in the latest fashions.

Impatient for action and wealth, Arnold decided to buy a ship and become a trader. He had sailed with his father and for Dr. Lathrop, and the idea of commanding his own ship thrilled him. He persuaded his sister, Hannah, to come to New Haven and manage his apothecary shop while he was away. Three years younger than Benedict, Hannah was completely devoted to him and remained so for the rest of her life.

Hannah was one of the few women in New Haven to run a shop. In eighteenth-century American cities, some women owned and managed businesses such as taverns, inns, and newspapers. But most women who earned an income, did so out of their homes. Some of them spun wool, for example. In rural areas, farm women traded dairy products.

Benedict Arnold was a large man with a strong personality.

Captain Arnold

As captain, Arnold felt at home on his ship. He was taller than average with a muscular build, and he had a forceful personality. Arnold seemed born to command. He proved to be a shrewd trader, and made frequent trips to Canada to trade goods for horses. He then traded the horses at a handsome profit to plantation owners in the West Indies.

By the time he was in his mid-twenties, Arnold owned three ships and the apothecary shop. In 1767, he married Margaret "Peggy" Mansfield, and over the next five years, the couple had three sons—Benedict, Richard, and Henry.

During his long trading voyages, he sent many letters to Peggy telling her how much he missed her. "Oh, when shall we be so happy to meet and part no more," he wrote. But Arnold's voyages were very profitable. He was one of Connecticut's wealthiest young merchants.

The British Tax the Colonists

Although Arnold's businesses were successful, he and his fellow merchants often suffered financially because of new British policies toward the colonies. The Seven Years' War had left Great Britain with a huge debt and a greatly expanded empire to defend. To King George III and his ministers in Parliament, it seemed only reasonable that the American colonies share in this financial burden.

Between 1763 and 1773, the British passed a series of laws to raise money from their American colonies: The colonists grumbled over the Quartering Act, passed in 1764, which re-quired them to provide barracks (sleeping quarters) and supplies for 10,000 British soldiers. They also objected to the Currency Act, which forced them to pay for imports with their shrinking supply of gold and silver instead of with paper currency. But it was the Stamp Act of 1765 that really angered them and touched off massive protests.

The Stamp Act required the colonists to pay a tax on many printed items—newspapers, legal documents, advertisements, and even playing cards. The colonists objected because this was a direct tax on the people that was imposed on them by British

Parliament. They were accustomed to paying taxes that were passed by their elected representatives in the Colonial assemblies (legislatures). Since the American colonists had no representatives in England's Parliament, they argued, Parliament had no right to tax them. "No taxation without representation!" became their rallying cry.

In October 1765, delegates from nine colonies met in New York to hold a Stamp Act Congress. It was a display of unity the colonies had never shown before. The congress sent a petition to Parliament, urging the repeal (withdrawal) of the Stamp Act. The colonies' unified action did not stop there. A determined minority of colonists, calling themselves Patriots, formed societies called the Sons of Liberty and Daughters of Liberty. The Daughters of Liberty urged people to boycott (stop purchasing) British imported goods and rely on their own handmade products. The Sons of Liberty made life miserable for the British stamp agents, who collected the taxes on paper goods. The Sons of Liberty beat up several agents, threatened others, and wrecked the agents' offices. Before the end of the year, every agent resigned.

The British gave in to the colonists' pressure and repealed (abolished) the Stamp Act early in 1766. Parliament, however, immediately passed a Declaratory Act, which insisted on Parliament's authority to make laws for the colonies "in all cases whatsoever."

Over the next decade, the conflict between the colonies and Great Britain followed a similar pattern. King George III and Parliament would issue new tax laws, demanding that the colonies accept these taxes from "their mother country" as grateful and obedient "children." The colonists protested each new measure (action), insisting on their right to have tax laws passed by their own representatives.

New Haven's Son of Liberty

Arnold and other merchants were troubled by new rules that made smuggling difficult. Colonial merchants traditionally avoided paying customs duties (taxes on imports) by paying a small bribe to a customs clerk. This practice was a form of smuggling. Now merchants suspected of smuggling risked having their ships searched by British naval officers. Those accused of the crime would be tried by a British judge rather than a Colonial jury. The Patriots felt that traditional British rights, like a trial by a jury of one's peers, were being taken away from them.

Arnold became a member of the New Haven Sons of Liberty. He was in a Caribbean port when he learned of the first act of violence committed by the British. In March 1770, British soldiers in Boston fired on a restless mob of colonists, killing five of them. Arnold shared the Patriots' outrage over what became known as the "Boston Massacre," and he favored an active response. "Good God!" he wrote to a friend, "are Americans all asleep and tamely giving up their glorious liberties?"

A Crisis Over Tea

The Boston Massacre was followed by a period of calm. Then in 1773, the British passed a law called the Tea Act. This act ultimately set off a chain of events that led to the American Revolution.

The Tea Act actually lowered the price of tea, the favorite Colonial beverage. But it gave a monopoly (exclusive control) on the tea trade to the British East India Company. Patriots saw this act as the first step in a British plan to gain control of all Colonial business. When the first shiploads of tea arrived, the Sons of Liberty in every Colonial port either locked the tea in warehouses or forced the ships to turn back.

On December 16, 1773, Patriots disguised as Mohawk warriors dumped chests of tea into the harbor. Their action became known as the "Boston Tea Party."

In Boston, the Sons of Liberty staged a more dramatic protest. Disguised as Mohawk warriors, they boarded a ship carrying tea and dumped 342 chests of it into Boston Harbor.

While many Patriots cheered the "Boston Tea Party," King George III and Parliament were furious. Early in 1774, they responded with a series of measures called the Coercive Acts. They were designed to punish Massachusetts, with the hope that the other colonies would become more cooperative in order to avoid a similar fate. The Port of Boston was closed until the Patriots paid for the tea, and Massachusetts lost most of its rights to govern itself. General Thomas Gage was sent to Boston with more troops. He was to be the colony's new military governor.

The colonists reacted to what they called the "Intolerable Acts" with an even greater determination to unite and resist British tyranny. Delegates from every colony but Georgia met in Philadelphia in September 1774 as the First Continental Congress. The delegates passed a series of resolutions, demanding that the British repeal the Coercive Acts. In the meantime, the delegates declared a boycott on all trade with Great Britain. They agreed to meet again the following May if their demands were not met.

The Opening Shots of the American Revolution

Through the tension-filled winter of 1774–1775, Colonial assemblies ordered towns to drill their militia units. Some of the units were called "Minutemen," who would be ready to fight at a moment's notice.

Arnold's Foot Guards

In New Haven, Benedict Arnold and his friends received permission to form their own militia company and called it "the Governor's Second Company of Foot Guards." As their captain, Arnold organized the 60 men into a well-disciplined unit. He couldn't resist outfitting the soldiers in dazzling uniforms, with scarlet coats, white breeches, and black leggings.

On April 20, 1775, an exhausted messenger rode into New Haven with news that battles had been fought the day before at Lexington and Concord, outside Boston. General Gage had sent a regiment of British troops to seize Patriot weapons stored at Concord. The British were met at Lexington, and then at Concord, by Minutemen from the surrounding towns. By the time the

On April 19, 1775, American militia fought the British at the battle of Lexington, shown below, and then at Concord.

British staggered back to Boston, they had suffered heavy losses from Colonial militiamen. Thousands more militiamen were camped outside Boston, trapping the British inside the city. The American Revolution had begun.

At an emergency town meeting, New Haven residents voted not to send the town's militia because they did not wish to commit an act of rebellion. Arnold and his Foot Guards ignored the vote, however, and prepared to march to Massachusetts on April 21. When a town official refused to open the town warehouse and give them gunpowder, Arnold flew into a rage. "Our friends and neighbors are being mowed down by redcoats [British soldiers]," he thundered. "Give us the powder or we will take it.... None but Almighty God shall prevent me from marching!" An hour later, Arnold's brightly clothed guards were on the road to Cambridge (near Boston), where the Patriots had organized a temporary government for Massachusetts.

Adventure at Fort Ticonderoga

When Arnold and his men arrived, the Patriots were trying to develop a strategy for keeping the British in Boston. They needed cannons, however, and Arnold had a solution. On his trading trips to Canada, he had stopped at Fort Ticonderoga, an old French fort on Lake Champlain. He knew there were many British cannons in the fort and only a handful of soldiers guarding them. He would lead an attack on the fort and seize the cannons.

Arnold was made the colonel of this secret mission, and he was given money to hire volunteers in western Massachusetts to attack the fort. On May 3, 1775, Arnold set off. His assignment was a dream come true: a bold military adventure that he would command. After leaving a recruiter in western Massachusetts to assemble his volunteers, he went on to Fort Ticonderoga by himself.

Ethan Allen enters the fort at Ticonderoga, startling a guard.

Unfortunately for Arnold, the mission to Ticonderoga did not turn out as he hoped it would. Members of the Connecticut legislature had also sent an expedition. At the head of this rival force was Ethan Allen, who led a rough band of woodsmen called the Green Mountain Boys. When Arnold caught up with them and insisted on taking command, the Green Mountain Boys laughed. Since he was alone, and Allen had more than 200 men, Arnold was forced to swallow his pride and accept a joint command with Allen.

In the pre-dawn hours of May 10, 1775, Benedict Arnold and Ethan Allen led 83 men into the massive, star-shaped fort. A single sentry tried to sound an alarm, but the rest of the fort's

47 defenders were asleep. The fort's commander realized that he had no choice but to surrender. The fort and more than 80 cannons fell into American hands.

Arnold soon found that he could not control the Green Mountain Boys. He was nearly shot when he tried to stop them from looting (stealing) supplies at the fort. With a handful of his own men, he armed a boat and sailed 100 miles up Lake Champlain, where he led an attack on the town of St. John, in British Canada. Arnold and his men also captured the only British warship on the lake and sailed it back to Ticonderoga. During his trip to Canada, he had acquired some useful information: There were only about 1,000 British soldiers in all of Canada. Arnold was eager to get back to the colonies to try and organize an invasion.

Preparing for War

On the same day that Benedict Arnold and Ethan Allen stormed into Fort Ticonderoga, Colonial delegates met in Philadelphia as the Second Continental Congress. The delegates now had a war to deal with, and they needed a strategy for waging it against the world's greatest military power. They voted to create a Continental Army out of the best militiamen camped outside Boston. George Washington, of Virginia, would be the commander in chief. He had fought as a brigadier in the Seven Years' War.

Before Washington could reach Boston, the Patriots clashed with the British again on June 17. In the course of the fight, which became known as the battle of Bunker Hill, the British forced the Patriots to retreat. But the British—who were nick-named the "redcoats" because of their crimson dress—suffered heavy losses. Americans were thrilled that their militiamen had successfully fought a professional army.

When Washington arrived in Cambridge, he began the task of organizing some of the eager, but poorly trained, militia into a Continental Army. "Never," he wrote, "has such a rabble been distinguished by the name of army." He appointed Henry Knox, a Boston bookseller, to go to Fort Ticonderoga and find a way to haul the captured cannons to the hills overlooking Boston.

Arnold Returns Home

On his way home, Arnold stopped in Albany, New York, where he received shocking news: His wife, Peggy, had died suddenly five days earlier. At age 34, Benedict Arnold found himself a widower with three young sons.

When Arnold arrived in New Haven, he was relieved to find that Hannah had matters well in hand. She had arranged Peggy's funeral, kept the businesses going, and was managing the household, including the three boys.

A storm of controversy over Fort Ticonderoga distracted Arnold from his personal troubles. He learned that Ethan Allen had sent reports of the fort's capture, emphasizing his own heroism and making no mention of Arnold's help. To make matters worse, conflicts arose over which colony should take charge of the fort until Congress could look into the matter. Arnold was not needed or wanted. Discouraged, Arnold broke up his force and resigned from his military appointment on June 24. But three weeks later, Arnold had bounced back. He was headed for Cambridge again, this time to discuss with General Washington his ideas for invading Canada.

Chapter 2

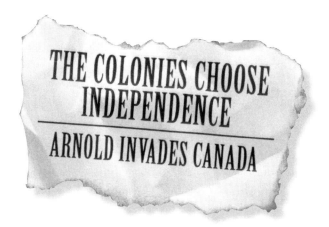

THE COLONIES CHOOSE
INDEPENDENCE

ARNOLD INVADES CANADA

*O*n August 15, 1775, Arnold met with General Washington in Cambridge. Washington had already decided to invade Canada, and Congress had ordered General Philip Schuyler to organize an army in Albany, New York, for that purpose. Schuyler's force was to invade Canada along the Hudson River–Lake Champlain waterway and attack Quebec, which was the capital of Canada.

Arnold proposed leading a second army through the Maine wilderness, and traveling on rivers and lakes wherever possible. His army would then cross the St. Lawrence River and march on Quebec. The commander in chief immediately approved the plan. The two invading armies would force the British to divide their defensive forces. If the Americans could capture Quebec, they would control the most populated region of Canada. It would be impossible for the British to launch an invasion from the North.

Washington hoped that the French citizens of Canada who objected to British rule would join the war, perhaps as America's fourteenth colony.

By the time he left for Canada on September 15, Arnold was a colonel in the Continental Army, in command of 1,080 eager volunteers. He selected a big, barrel-chested Virginian named Daniel Morgan to be one of his commanders. Morgan brought along a regiment of Virginia riflemen, who were later nicknamed "Morgan's Rifles."

Invasion

Arnold's expedition almost immediately encountered problems. The only map of northern Maine in existence contained huge errors; the distance from the Kennebec River to the St. Lawrence turned out to be twice the distance shown on the map. The 200 shallow-water boats Arnold had ordered for the trip presented even greater problems. They were crudely made boats, and within the first days on the Kennebec River, all of them were leaking badly. Arnold's food supplies were ruined. He described the scene in a letter to Washington.

> *When you consider the badness and weight of the bateaux* [boats] *and large quantities of provisions, etc., we have been obliged to force up against a very rapid stream, you would have taken the men for amphibious animals…*

Day after day, the men plunged deeper into the wilderness of Maine, carrying the clumsy boats from one body of water to the next. By the third week, the march turned into a desperate struggle for survival. The sounds of their approach frightened away the wild game that might have replaced the ruined food.

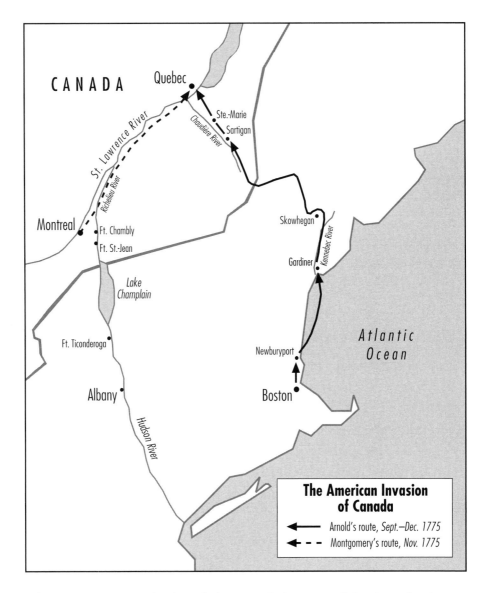

The American Invasion of Canada

← Arnold's route, *Sept.–Dec. 1775*

←-- Montgomery's route, *Nov. 1775*

The men soon cooked and devoured the expedition's only dog and, after that, "the shaving soap...lip salve...leather cartridge boxes, and candles." Eventually, Private Abner Stocking wrote, "when we arose to march in the morning many of the men were so weak that they could hardly stand.... When we attempted to march, they reeled about like drunken men, having now been without provisions for five days."

Arnold went ahead to get help. Just when it seemed that the men would all die in the wilderness, he returned with 18 friendly Canadians and some food. The army, reduced by desertions and deaths to less than 700 men, was saved. Although Arnold said little about his own role in this survival story, his men had nothing but praise for his "invincible courage."

Arnold's gaunt and ragged army was in no condition to attack Quebec, a walled fortress city perched on a cliff high above the St. Lawrence River. He led his men to within a few miles of the city and waited for General Schuyler's army to meet them.

That expedition had also run into difficulties. Schuyler had become too ill to continue and turned command over to General Richard Montgomery. After capturing the town of Montreal, Montgomery's men finally reached Quebec on December 3.

Montgomery and Arnold knew their only chance was to attack as soon as possible. They could not wait until spring because as soon as the ice broke up on the St. Lawrence, British warships and troop reinforcements would arrive.

The two commanders divided their forces and launched an assault during a blinding snowstorm on the night of December 31, 1775. Montgomery led his men along a narrow path up the front of the cliff beneath the city. A single volley of cannon and musket fire crashed into their ranks, killing Montgomery and 14 others. Montgomery's second in command was unable to keep the men from scrambling frantically down the cliff in a retreat.

Unaware of what had happened to Montgomery, Arnold led his men into narrow, twisting streets just outside the fortress walls of Quebec. Musket fire coming from the direction of the wall hit the Americans, and Arnold was wounded in the leg. While his boot filled with blood, Arnold urged his men on, telling them to follow Daniel Morgan. "He was still shouting," one soldier recalled, "in a cheering voice as we passed, urging us forward."

Arnold, General Richard Montgomery, and their men attacked Quebec during a blinding snowstorm on December 31, 1775.

BENEDICT ARNOLD AND THE AMERICAN REVOLUTION

Arnold dragged himself to a field hospital, and Morgan led the men over the walls and into the fortress. Without support from Montgomery's force, however, the assault was doomed. By mid-morning the Americans were surrounded. Morgan surrendered the 400 men under his command.

The battle for Quebec was over, and the defeat ended all hope of an American conquest of Canada. Arnold stubbornly insisted on waiting until spring, hoping to renew the attack. He wrote to his sister Hannah, "I have no thought of leaving this proud town, until I first enter it in triumph." In the meantime, he was moved to Montreal to recover from his wound. While he was there, he was pleased to learn that the Congress had promoted him to the rank of brigadier general.

Four hundred miles to the south, Washington had greater success with the Continental Army and militia outside Boston. Early in 1776, Henry Knox had arrived with 60 cannons from Fort Ticonderoga. The cannons were rapidly put in position on the heights overlooking Boston. The Americans' defensive position was now so strong that the British gave up Boston. A new British commander, General William Howe, replaced Gage and ordered a British evacuation of the city. In March 1776, thousands of Patriots cheered and wept with joy as the British fleet sailed out of sight, heading for Halifax, Canada. Washington guessed that after his return to a base in Canada, Howe would strike next at New York City. The American general immediately began moving his army south to meet that threat.

America Declares Independence

When the colonists first took up arms in April 1775, they were not thinking of independence. They were fighting to defend their rights as British citizens. In fact, Washington proposed a toast to King George III every evening that he remained in headquarters outside of Boston in 1775.

By the spring of 1776, however, the Patriots' mood had changed. John Adams, a Massachusetts delegate to the Continental Congress, expressed the feelings of many colonists when he wrote, "Britain has at last driven America to the last step, complete separation from her." In June, the Congress appointed a committee of five to prepare a draft of a declaration of independence.

The Declaration of Independence, written primarily by Thomas Jefferson of Virginia, was approved by the Congress on the evening of July 2, 1776. This eloquent document declared that the 13 colonies were now free and independent states, and it expressed their highest ideals:

> We hold these truths to be self-evident, that all men are created equal, that they are endowed by their creator with certain inalienable rights, that among these are life, liberty, and the pursuit of happiness.

Declaring independence was a bold step, one that no other colonial people had ever tried. Before the declaration was approved, Abigail Adams wrote to her husband, John, outlining some of the hard questions Americans faced:

> If we separate from Britain, what code of laws will be established? How shall we be governed so as to retain our liberties? Can any government be free which is not administered by general stated laws? Who shall frame these laws? Who will give them force and energy?
> When I consider these things…I feel anxious for the fate of our monarchy or democracy or whatever is to take place.

The Declaration of Independence was signed by members of the Continental Congress in July 1776.

Abigail Adams

Throughout the American Revolution, countless women like Abigail Adams took care of family business affairs while their husbands were on battlefields or working in a legislature. While her husband attended the Continental Congress, Abigail Adams operated the family farm in Massachusetts, managed the family's finances, and raised their five children. Like many Patriot women, she wanted the new government that was forming to recognize the contributions of women. While she did not go so far as to advocate full political equality and the right to vote, she did admonish her husband to "remember the ladies, and be more generous and favorable to them than your ancestors."

Challenges Ahead

The Declaration of Independence created 13 independent states, but there was no strong central government to make the states truly united. The Continental Congress was directing the war effort, but it had little authority over the states, except for the right to demand their contributions of soldiers and money.

Another difficulty was that Americans had different opinions about the war. Out of a population of 2.5 million, an estimated 1 million were Patriots, another 1 million did not take a stand, and roughly 500,000 were Loyalists who opposed the Revolution.

The Loyalists, who were also known as Tories (named after Britain's ruling Tory party), made up a majority of the population in Georgia and the Carolinas. An estimated 50,000 Loyalists fought on the British side, forming their own regiments.

The British, too, faced problems. They were fighting a war an ocean away from their homeland, and nearly all their supplies—including cannons, ammunition, and horses—had to be transported across the Atlantic. The British commanders also had trouble recruiting solders. Many Englishmen and women regarded the Revolution as a civil war between British subjects (citizens of a monarchy). To fill the army's ranks, the king was forced to hire troops, called "mercenaries," from Europe's German states. A total of around 30,000 German mercenaries fought in the American Revolution.

⁓ THE DECLARATION AND AFRICAN AMERICANS ⁓

The Declaration of Independence seemed to hold out special hope for African Americans. They were encouraged by the Declaration's ringing words, proclaiming that "all men are created equal, that they are endowed with certain inalienable rights, that among these are life, liberty, and the pursuit of happiness." Many African Americans felt that the new nation should live up to its stated ideals and abolish slavery. One group, which included several slaves, signed a petition stating, "We have in common with all other men a natural right to that freedom which the Great Parent of the universe has bestowed equally on all mankind."

Although the Declaration of Independence was a remarkably democratic document for the eighteenth century, Americans of European heritage were not yet ready to end slavery or to extend the ideal of equality to non-white peoples. It was not until 1776 that Washington allowed free African Americans to enlist in the army. About 5,000 eventually served in the army, and 2,000 more in the navy. The British were less hesitant and often granted freedom to slaves who joined the British cause. Nearly 15,000 freed slaves left the country with the British, including 3 who had been Washington's slaves.

Although slavery was not abolished until the Civil War (1861–1865), the northern states began outlawing slavery soon after the Revolution. In 1787, the Congress responded by prohibiting slavery from new lands on the nation's northwestern frontier.

Defeat, Retreat, and a Surprise

While the Continental Congress was debating the Declaration of Independence, British General Howe launched a massive invasion of New York City. More than 400 ships landed 32,000 redcoats and German mercenaries on Staten Island. Through July and August of 1776, they steadily pushed Washington's forces out of Long Island, near New York City, and eventually took control of the city itself, as hundreds of frightened militiamen fled.

During the autumn of 1776, Washington retreated steadily through New Jersey and across the Delaware River into Pennsylvania. His primary goal was to avoid an all-out battle that could destroy the remains of his Continental Army and probably end the Revolution. When American morale seemed at its lowest point, Washington made a surprise move. He led his men across the ice-clogged Delaware River on Christmas night and overwhelmed a German mercenary base in Trenton, New Jersey. He then marched onto Princeton, where he beat the British on January 3, 1777, forcing them out of most of New Jersey. Washington led his exhausted troops into winter quarters at Morristown, New Jersey.

Arnold Confronts the British

During the summer and autumn of 1776, Arnold joined the American retreat from Canada. As the Americans traveled south, the British prepared to launch an invasion by way of Lake Champlain. At Fort Ticonderoga, Arnold received permission to have a fleet of small ships built to sail on Lake Champlain. He wanted to slow down the British advance.

In a matter of weeks, Arnold and his 16 new ships traveled north on the lake. On October 11, 1776, they met the British fleet near Valcour Island, near the middle of the lake. In two days of fighting, Arnold lost most of his small fleet, but the British suffered such heavy losses that they returned to Canada. This naval battle forced the British to delay their invasion nearly a year, giving the Americans precious time to prepare.

Wounded Pride

While Arnold was home in New Haven during the winter of 1776–1777, he was treated like a military hero. His glory, however, did not last long. Early in 1777, Arnold learned that the Continental Congress had promoted five men to the rank of major general, a position that was superior to his. None of the five could match Arnold's experience or achievements.

Arnold was given a horse for his bravery in fighting at Danbury, Connecticut.

Angry about this new development, Arnold decided in April that he would go to Philadelphia and discuss the matter with the Congress. But just as he was preparing to leave, a British force landed on the Connecticut coast and destroyed American supplies stored at Danbury, not far from New Haven. Arnold rushed to Danbury to help. In a sharp, two-day battle, he once again displayed his amazing courage. His horse was shot while he was riding, and he was nearly captured. But Arnold kept up the attack. After suffering heavy casualties, the British gave up and reboarded their ships.

In Philadelphia, the Congress presented Arnold with a horse to thank him for his latest "gallant action" at Danbury. It also promoted him to major general, but he was still junior to the five men they had recently appointed.

Benedict Arnold's enormous pride was still not satisfied. He insisted on being made senior to the other five major generals. When the Congress refused to give in, Arnold submitted a letter of resignation on July 11, 1777. On the same day, however, the Congress received a letter from General Washington, reporting that the British had launched a major invasion from Canada.

The commander in chief urged Congress to send Arnold north to help meet the invasion. "He is active, judicious, and brave," Washington wrote, "and an officer in whom the militia will repose the greatest confidence.... I have no doubt of his adding much to the honors he has already acquired." The Congress agreed, and refused Arnold's letter of resignation.

Arnold immediately set off for Albany, New York, to prepare for a confrontation with the British. It would be one of the most important battles of the American Revolution.

Chapter 3

TURNING POINT AT SARATOGA
A LEADER WITH COURAGE

$\mathcal{B}$y the time Benedict Arnold reached the American forces under General Schuyler near Albany, New York, the British invasion was well underway. British General Burgoyne was launching a three-part invasion. Burgoyne himself led the main army of nearly 10,000 British soldiers, German mercenaries, and Canadian Loyalists, along with several hundred Native American warriors. A smaller army was advancing from the west, through the Mohawk River Valley. The third part of the assault was to be provided by General Howe, who was to move up the Hudson River from New York City. When all three armies met at Albany, the British would have control of the entire Hudson River–Lake Champlain waterway, stretching from New York City to Canada. New England would be cut off from the other states, and the Revolution would soon collapse. Or so the British thought.

Burgoyne's army covered the length of Lake Champlain. They easily recaptured Fort Ticonderoga from the Americans, and by August 1, 1777, they were less than 50 miles north of Albany. The second force, traveling eastward under Colonel Barry St. Leger, crossed Lake Ontario and marched toward Albany. St. Leger's 450 regulars (soldiers), joined by 1,000 Iroquois warriors, surrounded Fort Stanwix, on the Mohawk River.

British General John Burgoyne's plan for a three-part invasion of the northeastern states began to unravel during the summer of 1777.

Problems for Burgoyne

With only 4,500 men under his command, Schuyler did his best to prepare for the British assault. He sent teams of woodsmen north to slow Burgoyne's advance. The men felled trees and created dams to block the primitive paths through New York's dense forests. The British could barely advance a mile a day. They travelled with the wives and children of several hundred officers, and they were burdened by tons of baggage, food, cannons, and ammunition.

As soon as Arnold arrived, Schuyler asked him to lead an expedition of 900 men to support the Americans at Fort Stanwix. As Arnold marched toward the surrounded fort, he worried that he did not have enough men, and he decided to try a trick. Arnold sent a Loyalist prisoner named Hon-Yost Schuyler (no relation to the general) to go to the enemy and report an untrue story. Hon-Yost told the British that he had just escaped from Arnold, who was approaching with an army of thousands. The story, supported by two friendly Native Americans, was convincing enough to persuade the many Iroquois fighting with St. Leger to flee. After seeing two-thirds of his army disappear, St. Leger felt he had no choice but to return to Canada. One branch of Burgoyne's three-part invasion was gone.

At almost the same time, Burgoyne suffered another serious loss. He sent a force of 900 German mercenaries into present-day Vermont to seize American supplies stored at Bennington. On August 16, 1777, a force of 2,000 militiamen under General John Stark overwhelmed the mercenaries, killing 200 and capturing 700. The total loss amounted to about one-tenth of Burgoyne's army.

There was more bad news from New York. Burgoyne learned that General Howe was not coming north. Instead, Howe had decided to attack Washington's main Continental Army and seize Philadelphia. On September 11, 1777, Howe's 18,000-man army defeated the Continentals at the battle of Brandywine Creek, in New Jersey. Two weeks later, Howe entered Philadelphia. The Continental Congress was on the run, fleeing first to the town of York, and then to Lancaster.

Although Burgoyne was stunned by Howe's change of plans, he saw a glimmer of hope. Howe had left General Henry Clinton in charge at New York City, with orders to help Burgoyne if necessary. Burgoyne sent an urgent message to Clinton, asking him to send a force up the Hudson River. Even if Clinton did not come, Burgoyne remained confident that his well-trained army could defeat whatever American troops stood between him and Albany.

Propaganda is the use of words and pictures to influence people's opinions. This form of persuasion played an important role in the American Revolution. A striking example occurred in March 1770, after British soldiers fired into a mob of Boston residents, killing five people. Patriot leader Samuel Adams labeled the incident the "Boston Massacre." Paul Revere's engraving of the event was reproduced in Colonial newspapers, fanning the flames of anti-British feeling.

The Patriot Thomas Paine became famous for the most important piece of propaganda that was written during the Revolution. In a pamphlet called *Common Sense*, he presented clear, logical arguments in favor of independence. Paine wrote, "[Independence] means no more than this: whether we shall make our own laws, or whether the king... shall tell us, *There shall be no laws but such as I like.*" The pamphlet sold more than 150,000 copies in only a few months, and encouraged many Americans to consider breaking away from their "mother country."

Americans were also very good at spreading propaganda orally. In 1777, some Patriots told their fellow colonists that General Burgoyne paid Native American warriors to kill colonists and bring him the scalps. This was not true, of course. But in July 1777, a young woman named Jane McCrea was kidnapped and killed by three warriors who were loyal to Burgoyne. Accounts of "the murder of Jane McCrea" spread through the states. The story made the false tales of money for American scalps believable. Many angry militiamen joined the battle of Saratoga in response to the McCrea murder.

The First Battle of Saratoga

Arnold returned to the Albany region after his clever rescue of Fort Stanwix. When he arrived, he found that his friend Schuyler had been replaced by General Horatio Gates. A long-time rival of Schuyler's, Gates had convinced the Continental Congress that Schuyler was responsible for the loss of Ticonderoga and should be removed from his command. The scheming Gates was cordial to Arnold and placed him in command of one wing of his army. He had never trusted Arnold, however, and these two ambitious men would soon clash.

An engraving of the Boston Massacre by Paul Revere helped create support for the Patriots.

Gates moved his army to a place called Bemis Heights, about 25 miles north of Albany and about 10 miles from the town of Saratoga. The Americans established their defenses on some heavily wooded hills overlooking the Hudson. They built very strong fortifications and artillery emplacements (positions) under the guidance of Colonel Thaddeus Kosciuszko, a Polish volunteer and talented military engineer.

The American forces grew steadily as more militia units arrived. Washington had sent some of his best men, including Colonel Daniel Morgan and his 600 "Morgan's Rifles," who had attempted an invasion of Canada along with Arnold.

Horatio Gates feuded with Arnold during the battle of Saratoga.

Morgan had been released from captivity in a prisoner exchange, and he was pleased to be under the command of his old friend Benedict Arnold.

On the morning of September 19, 1777, Burgoyne's troops moved cautiously through the thick woods toward the American defenses. Arnold persuaded Gates to let him send Morgan's Rifles to test the enemy's strength. Morgan's men ran into the main British column at a clearing called Freeman's Farm, touching off a fierce battle that lasted all day.

Arnold rushed into the battle with reinforcements. Continental Captain Ebenezer Wakefield recalled, "Nothing could exceed the bravery of Arnold on this day. He seemed the very genius of war." First one side and then the other gained control of the clearing. British bayonets (rifles with knives fastened to them) had the advantage at close range, while Morgan's expert riflemen were deadly at a distance. As the autumn dusk approached, a German mercenary regiment raced up the hill to stop the last American attack of the day. The battle ended with no clear winner, but the British had suffered 620 casualties. That was more than twice the number of American losses. The Americans were pleased that they had blunted an attack by some of the best troops in King George's army.

The Second Battle of Saratoga

Burgoyne planned to renew his attack the next day, but he decided to wait after receiving word that General Clinton planned to move north from New York City with 4,000 men. Burgoyne sent a messenger to Clinton, urging him to hurry. Then he ordered his men to build sturdy log barricades, called "redoubts," in a semi-circle surrounding the main British camp. Two weeks passed with no word from Clinton. Burgoyne did not realize that his messenger had been captured. Clinton was totally unaware of Burgoyne's need for support.

By early October, the British were in a desperate position. Hundreds of German mercenaries and all of Burgoyne's Native American warriors deserted. He now had around 6,000 men, and they were forced to survive on half-rations because food supplies were so low. Facing Burgoyne was an American army that now numbered over 11,000.

On the American side, Arnold's feud with Gates was creating tension. In reporting on the first battle of Saratoga to the Continental Congress, Gates made no mention of Arnold. He then infuriated his sensitive general further by removing Morgan's Rifles from Arnold's command and placing them under his own. Arnold demanded an explanation. The two men engaged in a heated shouting match, which ended when Arnold said he was leaving the camp. "Arnold's intention to quit this department... has caused great uneasiness among the soldiers," wrote Henry Brockholst Livingston, a member of Arnold's staff. The other officers persuaded Arnold to stay, but Gates had enough. He stripped Arnold of all command and ordered him to remain in camp once the fighting resumed.

On October 7, 1777, Burgoyne renewed his attack, leading 1,500 of his best men and about 600 Canadian Loyalists. When

Gates learned of the British movement, he ordered Morgan to advance on their left, and another regiment on the right. Both American forces struck at the same time, and the British fell back.

The sounds of the battle were too much for Arnold. Defying Gates's order, he leaped on his horse, jumped over a barrier, and sped toward the crashing sounds of muskets and small cannons.

Arnold was wounded at the second battle of Saratoga (shown here), after displaying extraordinary courage by charging the enemy on horseback.

BENEDICT ARNOLD AND THE AMERICAN REVOLUTION

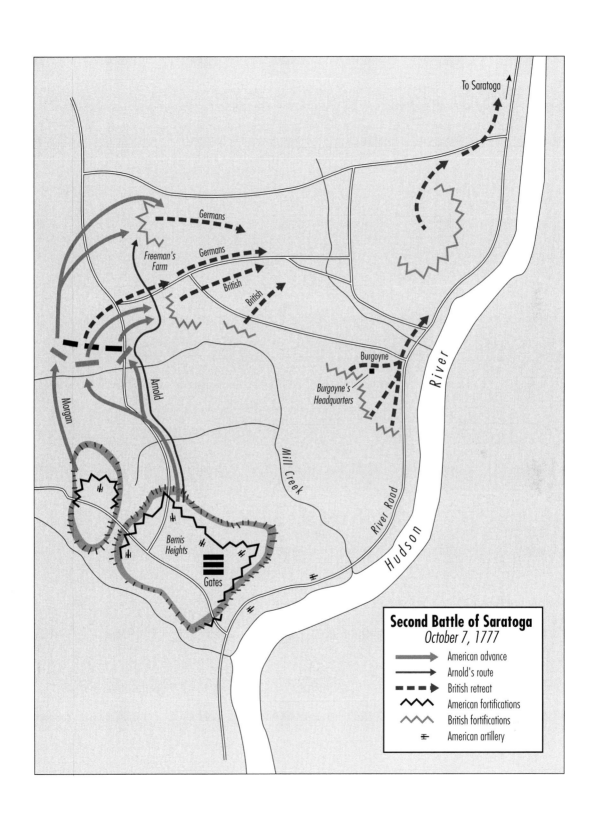

To Saratoga

Germans

Freeman's
Farm

Germans

British

British

Burgoyne

Burgoyne's
Headquarters

River

Morgan

Arnold

Mill Creek

River Road

Hudson

Bemis
Heights

Gates

Second Battle of Saratoga
October 7, 1777

→ American advance

→ Arnold's route

⇢ British retreat

∿∿ American fortifications

∿∿ British fortifications

⊞ American artillery

The men cheered when they saw him and eagerly followed as he took control of the battle.

The British and the German mercenaries retreated to the protection of two redoubts. Arnold led a charge against one of them. The British and Germans forced the Americans back, and Arnold headed for the other redoubt. Shouting "Victory or Death!" he rode between the opposing lines of redcoats and Americans, completely exposed to enemy fire. He gathered up more men near the second redoubt and led the way around it. Arnold's horse was hit several times, and Arnold barely managed to leap clear of it as the horse fell. A wounded German mercenary, who lay on the ground, fired at Arnold and hit him in the leg.

While Arnold lay writhing in pain, the Americans finished off the day's fighting, winning an overwhelming victory. More than 600 of Burgoyne's men were wounded or killed, compared with 150 American casualties. Morgan's men placed Arnold on a piece of tent canvas and carried him back to the American lines. One of the officers asked where he had been hit. "In the same leg," Arnold gasped through the pain. "I wish it had been my heart." He had been wounded in that leg during the Americans' invasion of Quebec.

Turning Point

Burgoyne finally ordered his beaten army to retreat, but they got only as far as the village of Saratoga. There, the British found themselves trapped by the swarming Continentals and militia. Burgoyne was forced to surrender on October 17, 1777.

The battle of Saratoga marked the turning point of the American Revolution, although four more years of struggle and bloodshed followed that victory. The surrender itself was astounding. Burgoyne gave up 7 generals, more than 300 other officers, 5,000 soldiers, and large quantities of weapons and ammunition. Throughout the 13 states, people's spirits soared as the news spread. Washington's troops had suffered another defeat near Philadelphia, but the Continental Army remained intact. The troops went into their winter quarters at Valley Forge feeling optimistic about winning the war.

The most important result of the battle was its affect on France. Benjamin Franklin and other diplomats had been trying to persuade the French to join the war against their old enemy, Great Britain. The smashing victory at Saratoga convinced the French that the Americans could win. In February 1778, France signed a treaty of alliance, recognizing American independence and declaring war on Great Britain.

Benjamin Franklin helped to persuade the French to become allies in the war.

When Washington received the news, he proclaimed "a day of rejoicing throughout the whole army." The Americans looked forward to the help of the French army and navy, along with the desperately needed supplies they would bring.

Chapter 4

THE SHIFTING FORTUNES OF WAR

ARNOLD IS COURT-MARTIALED

*A*fter his heroism at Saratoga, Benedict Arnold faced a long, painful recovery from his wound. He managed to fight off the doctors who wanted to amputate the leg, but the wound left him with a severe limp. The shattered leg was 2 inches shorter than his other leg.

While he was recovering at home during the winter of 1777–1778, Arnold learned that the Continental Congress was hailing General Gates as the "hero of Saratoga." Gates's report of the second battle again made no mention of Arnold, other than to say he had been wounded.

At his winter quarters at Valley Forge, George Washington was also having trouble with the Congress. His troops were suffering through a bitterly cold winter without adequate food, clothing, or shelter. Local farmers gave what help they could, but they had sold their surplus crops at harvest time, leaving them with only enough food to see their families through the winter. Even before winter had fully set in, Washington wrote that "for some days past, there has been little less than famine in camp." The commander in chief made many appeals to the Continental Congress for such essentials as food, coats, and shoes. Nearly 3,000 soldiers died of exposure to the weather, of starvation, or of illness.

WASHINGTON AND THE "CONWAY CABAL"

Benedict Arnold was not the only general who had problems with fellow officers. Even the nation's commander in chief had some strong opponents in high places. One murky plot against Washington became known as the "Conway Cabal" (the Conway Conspiracy).

Shortly after the battle of Saratoga, Washington was told of a letter written to General Horatio Gates by General Thomas Conway, a French-born officer with friends in the Continental Congress. Conway's letter accused Washington of incompetence and hinted that Gates should replace him. Washington was shocked and angry about what he had learned, but he waited calmly for evidence.

A few weeks later, the Congress made Gates head of the Board of War, which supervised the operations of the Continental Army. Conway was promoted to major general. He was also given a new position— inspector general of the army. As the inspector general, Conway reported directly to the Board of War. It is not clear how far this plot went, or even whether it actually was a plot to remove Washington from his position as commander in chief. But it seems clear that some members of the Congress packed the Board of War with men opposed to Washington.

In February 1778, Washington wrote scathing letters to all those

George Washington

involved. Gates professed innocence, and Conway was forced to resign from the army. The conspiracy, if it actually existed, seemed to vanish.

A New British Strategy

The British were shaken by their terrible defeat at the battle of Saratoga, and by France's entry into the war. They decided to try a different military strategy. General Henry Clinton, the new commander of the British forces, was ordered to abandon Philadelphia and concentrate his army in New York City. From there, he was supposed to launch invasions of the southern states, where Loyalist sympathies were strongest. At the same time, the Royal Navy would establish a tight blockade of the entire American coast.

In June 1778, the Americans forced the British to evacuate Philadelphia. The redcoats took 3,000 Loyalists with them. Washington asked Arnold, now well enough to ride in a carriage, to become the military governor of the city. His job was to restore order after almost a year of British occupation.

Arnold entered Philadelphia a few days after the British left. In the meantime, Washington led his Continentals in pursuit of Clinton's army. The redcoats made it safely to New York City, and the Continental Army took up positions around it.

The Military Governor of Philadelphia

In June 1778, Arnold began two stormy years as military governor. During that time, he seemed to become embroiled in one controversy after another. From the beginning, many in the city were annoyed by the lifestyle he established for himself. He took over the mansion vacated by General Howe, and staffed it with personal servants as well as grooms and footmen for his fancy carriage. He entertained extravagantly, and he offended many Patriots by inviting as guests men and women suspected of having Loyalist sympathies.

Arnold's house in Philadelphia while he was military governor between 1778 and 1780.

Arnold also made enemies by trying to profit financially from his position. He had some of his men store valuable goods left behind by the Loyalists, so that he could sell them and keep the money. Other commanders on both sides of the conflict engaged in the same kind of war profiteering, but they did so more quietly. Arnold felt justified in making money, and he made no attempt to hide his activities. He had devoted himself to the Revolution for more than three years and still had received none of his pay from the Congress. His household expenses increased when he had Hannah and his three sons come to live with him.

There was still another drain on Arnold's finances. While he was military governor, he began courting 18-year-old Margaret "Peggy" Shippen. Attractive and well educated, Peggy was the daughter of a wealthy judge who was suspected of being a Loyalist. She was the darling of Philadelphia high society. As one British officer wrote before the redcoats evacuated, "We were all in love with her." Arnold and Peggy were married in April 1779, when Arnold was 38.

Building a New Nation

While militiamen tried to bring the Revolution to a victorious end on the battlefield, other Americans were busy building a new nation. The Declaration of Independence transformed 13 colonies into independent states. Now the leaders in each state immediately set to work to create new state governments. They approached this task in a spirit of democratic reform. The leaders believed that people and their elected representatives in the state legislatures should have the most political power. They thought the state's governor and the nation's central government should have less. By 1778, ten of the states had their constitutions in place. This was the first time in history that people had written constitutions stating exactly what powers the government would have. Each constitution also contained a bill of rights. It defined the citizens' basic rights, such as freedom of speech and of religion, which could not be taken away by any government.

The definition of who a state's citizens were also became more democratic. In some states it was no longer necessary to own property in order to vote. The framers did not intend to extend voting rights to women or to African Americans, however. But in New Jersey, some unclear wording in the constitution enabled some women and free blacks to vote. That "mistake" was corrected in 1807, however.

The American's distrust of a central authority (based on their experience with the King of England) made it difficult for them to create a strong national government. After months of debate, the Congress proposed a document called the Articles of Confederation. The Articles proclaimed that the Congress would be the only branch of government, and it would have few powers. The Congress would be able to wage war, make peace, and manage foreign affairs, including relations with Native American tribes.

But it could not raise money though taxation. And the Congress had no way to enforce any laws it passed. In 1781, the Articles were finally approved by all of the states. The Confederation government officially began, although the Congress had been directing war operations since 1775.

Trouble in Pennsylvania

In Pennsylvania, the men forming the government were irritated that the Congress had imposed a military governor on the state. As a result, they were critical of every move Arnold made. Arnold showed little respect for the new state leaders, which didn't help matters. When they accused him of abusing his powers, he complained to the Congress that they were "a set of wretches beneath the notice of a gentleman and man of honor."

In January 1779, the Pennsylvania government presented Congress with eight charges against Arnold for abusing his authority. Most members of the Congress were not impressed by the charges, but they also realized they could not risk losing the state's cooperation. After an all-night debate, the Congress voted to have Arnold court-martialed (tried in a military court).

Arnold felt betrayed by the Congress. Then he received a letter from Washington saying that the court-martial was being delayed and he would be informed of a date for the proceedings. The cool, formal tone of Washington's letter seemed to send Arnold into a panic. In the spring of 1779, he wrote a frantic letter to the commander in chief. "If your Excellency thinks me criminal," he pleaded, "for heaven's sake, let me be immediately tried and, if found guilty, executed." He had, he continued, "made every sacrifice of fortune and blood, and become a cripple in the service of my country.... I have nothing left but the little reputation I have gained in the army. Delay in the present case is worse than death."

Arnold Contacts the British

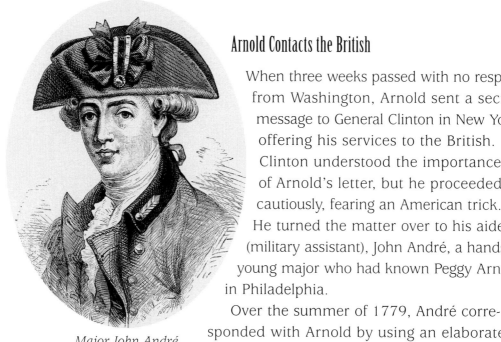

Major John André

When three weeks passed with no response from Washington, Arnold sent a secret message to General Clinton in New York, offering his services to the British. Clinton understood the importance of Arnold's letter, but he proceeded cautiously, fearing an American trick. He turned the matter over to his aide (military assistant), John André, a handsome young major who had known Peggy Arnold in Philadelphia.

Over the summer of 1779, André corresponded with Arnold by using an elaborate system of codes. Arnold, and occasionally Peggy, sent valuable information to André. For example, Arnold told André of Washington's plans to cooperate with the French army that had landed in Newport, Rhode Island.

"Imprudent and Improper"

After six months of delays, Arnold finally faced his fellow officers in a court-martial in January 1780. The court cleared him of most of the charges made by the Pennsylvania legislature, except for two: issuing passes to a ship's crew without authority, and using freight wagons belonging to the state of Pennsylvania to transport personal goods. Arnold's only punishment was to be a reprimand (scolding) from the commander in chief.

Arnold was relieved. A few words in private from Washington and the whole affair would be over. Instead, Washington felt he had to make the reprimand public. He declared that Arnold's use of the wagons was "imprudent and improper."

The commander in chief, knowing his overly sensitive general would feel wounded by the reprimand, wrote him a private letter, urging him to "exhibit anew those noble qualities which have placed you on the list of our most valued commanders." He promised to offer Arnold a new position that would give him "opportunities of regaining the esteem of your country," hinting that he might be the commander of West Point, an important fort on the Hudson River.

Defeats in the South

Washington needed Arnold's help because the nation's military fortunes had declined badly. Burgoyne's plan to concentrate on the South seemed to be working. The redcoats captured Savannah, Georgia, late in 1778. With the strong Loyalist support there, the British re-established a royal government in Georgia.

Then in the spring of 1780, the British captured Charleston, South Carolina, forcing 5,000 American defenders to surrender. General Clinton could proudly write to the British secretary of war: "I may venture to assert that there are a few men in South Carolina who are not either our prisoners or in arms with us." It was the worst American defeat of the war. Without consulting Washington, the Congress sent General Gates to take command in the South. In August 1780, Gates led the Americans into another disaster at the battle of Camden (South Carolina), where Gates himself fled the battlefield. An embarrassed Congress appointed a committee to investigate Gates's conduct and asked Washington to name a new southern commander.

In the meantime, Benedict Arnold prepared for the final betrayal of his country.

Chapter 5

AMERICA'S VICTORY
ARNOLD'S TREASON

*W*ashington met with Arnold in June 1780 to discuss military plans. Instead of offering Arnold the command at West Point, Washington asked him to take command of the army's entire left wing. The army was divided into three parts, and Washington commanded the center.

Both men knew this was a great honor for Arnold. It showed Washington's confidence in him, and the position would do much to restore Arnold's reputation. The commander in chief was stunned, therefore, when Arnold declined. Arnold said that his leg was still too painful for a field command post, and he would rather have the position at West Point. Washington was disappointed, but he reluctantly agreed.

The commander in chief did not know that Arnold had already made plans for West Point. Soon after Washington had first mentioned the possibility of a position there, Arnold wrote to André. Arnold made the astonishing offer to turn over to the British the fort and 4,000 Patriots in exchange for the sum of 20,000 pounds (about $600,000 in today's U.S. dollars). The British had agreed.

Arnold's Motives

Benedict Arnold turned down a chance to restore his honor by taking command of the Continental Army's left wing. Instead, he chose to betray his country. To this day, historians are still not certain why.

In June 1780, Arnold turned down an important military command because it conflicted with his plan to commit treason.

There are several explanations for Arnold's treason, although none of them provides a justification for what he did. The simplest is that he needed the money. His own fortune was gone, and he had not yet been paid for his four years of military service. Since he and Peggy Arnold enjoyed an extravagant lifestyle, money was important to him. In addition, he felt that despite his military accomplishments, the Congress treated him badly. His immense pride prevented him from seeing that he caused some of his wounds himself.

Arnold's actions can also be explained in terms of the very nature of the Revolution. Many people switched sides. Some did so out of a sense of commitment, and others for convenience. Both the British and the American armies had hundreds of soldiers who had deserted the other side. Some men and women switched sides more than once. For example, after declaring himself the Patriot hero of Fort Ticonderoga, Ethan Allen tried to make Vermont part of British Canada. When that plot failed, he rejoined the Patriot cause.

Arnold's own explanation for his treason was that he switched sides out of a sense of commitment to his country. A number of people supported the Revolution at the beginning of the war, and then decided that restoring ties with Great Britain was the only way to end years of bloodshed. A Loyalist newspaper published Arnold's defense of his actions. It was addressed "To the Inhabitants of America." Arnold claimed that the "reunion of the British Empire [was] the best and only means to dry up the streams of misery that have deluged this country." The British eventually proposed a peace plan that allowed Americans to have their own congress with the power to levy taxes. A leading Loyalist named Colonel Beverly Robinson wrote to Arnold, urging him to lead Americans toward a compromise with Britain. "Render, brave general, this important service to your country," Robinson wrote. "Let us put an end to so many calamities."

"Treason of the Blackest Dye"

In August 1780, Arnold took command at West Point and began putting his scheme of betrayal in motion. West Point was the main fort in a 15-mile chain of forts guarding the Hudson region. All of them were now under Arnold's control. His first step was to weaken West Point's defenses by sending the soldiers out in work crews to make repairs on the crumbling fortifications. By scattering the crews to different parts of the region, it would be difficult to re-assemble all 4,500 men in time to defend the fort if the British attacked.

In early September, around the time that Arnold was ready to proceed with his plan, Peggy arrived with their infant son. Arnold soon ran into two complications. He received a note from Washington that said he would stop at West Point on his way to Hartford to meet a French commander. A second obstacle was General Clinton's insistence that Arnold and Major André meet in person before Arnold executed his scheme.

Peggy Shippen Arnold and one of the Arnolds' children

Arnold wrote a note to Clinton suggesting that the redcoats could capture General Washington in addition to taking West Point, and he told Clinton where Washington would be staying. Clinton did not try to take Washington, however. Either the message did not arrive in time, or Clinton did not trust Arnold's information.

Arnold agreed to a personal meeting with André in late September. On the night of September 21, 1780, the British warship *Vulture* anchored on the Hudson River, near West Point, and André came ashore to meet Arnold. Clinton had given André strict instructions to remain in uniform and to carry no documents. During the night, however, an American guard at an outpost above the river opened fire on the *Vulture*, forcing it back downstream. André lost his transportation back to New York. After meeting with Arnold, he decided to put on a disguise and travel by land. Arnold provided him with a horse and wrote a pass, which André stuffed into his boot along with some papers from their meeting. Then he headed off.

The lower Hudson valley was a kind of no-man's land, roamed by tough gangs of Patriots and Loyalists. When André was stopped by a Patriot band of three men, he tried to talk his way past them, but his story made no sense to them. They decided to search him, hoping to find money. Instead, they found André's papers. The Patriots took André to a Continental Army officer named John Jameson. He decided to hold André as a prisoner and send the papers to Washington, who was on his way back from Hartford.

John André was caught with papers from his meeting with Arnold, including an estimate of the American forces at West Point.

BENEDICT ARNOLD AND THE AMERICAN REVOLUTION

A band of Patriots watches John André approach.

Jameson sent a second message to Arnold telling him he had a prisoner who claimed that Arnold signed his pass.

The Arnolds were at breakfast with Arnold's aides, waiting for Washington to arrive, when Jameson's messenger came. Arnold seemed outwardly calm as he took Peggy aside and told her what had happened. He then told his staff he had to go across the river but would be back soon. Arnold made a dash for the river, where he ordered the crew of his barge to row him downstream to the *Vulture*, the British warship.

When Washington and his staff arrived at West Point an hour later, they found Arnold's house in disorder. Arnold's aides had no idea what had happened, or why Peggy was in her room screaming hysterically. Then Jameson's second messenger arrived in search of Washington, carrying the papers that were found in André's boot. Washington looked at them in silence, his hands trembling. He quietly took one of Arnold's aides for a walk, told him of the treason, and returned to visit Peggy.

Peggy Arnold played her role so well that Washington's physician thought she would die. All of the men were convinced that she was an innocent victim of her husband's treason. Washington's aide, a young Alexander Hamilton, wrote to his fiancé, "Her sufferings were so eloquent that I wished myself her brother to have the right to become her defender." Washington sympathized with her and provided an escort to take her and the children to Philadelphia. He then called up reinforcements to strengthen the fort and placed General Nathanael Greene in command.

On September 26, 1780, Greene officially informed the army that "Treason of the blackest dye was yesterday discovered!" Washington ordered André brought to West Point, where a court-martial condemned him to death as a spy because he had not been wearing his uniform when captured. Arnold was safe with the British.

Both Arnold and Clinton wrote letters, urging Washington to spare André's life. Arnold warned that the commander in chief would be responsible "for the torrent of blood that may be spilt" if André was hanged. Washington was not moved, and Major

André was hanged. André, who had asked to be executed by a firing squad, faced the gallows with calm and dignity. "I pray you to bear me witness," he said to the officer in charge, "that I meet my fate like a brave man." He grabbed the noose from the executioner and put it in place himself. He was the highest-ranking officer executed during the war.

Word of Arnold's treason spread rapidly through a stunned nation. Down the streets of Philadelphia, an angry mob carted a crude-looking figure that looked like Arnold. Another crowd went into a cemetery in Norwich Town, Connecticut, to destroy the tombstones of Arnold's relatives.

⁓ OTHERS WHO BETRAYED THEIR COUNTRY ⁓

Other Americans were accused of betraying their country during the war, but none committed acts of treason that compared with Benedict Arnold's betrayal.

Silas Deane (1737–1789) was a leading Patriot who represented Connecticut in both the First and Second Continental Congresses. As a secret agent for the Patriots in France, he secured eight shiploads of guns and supplies for the American cause. But Deane gradually came to feel that reaching a compromise with Great Britain was best for the country, and he began writing letters to persuade friends. In the Congress, he was accused of disloyalty and of stealing American funds. Angry at how he was being treated, Deane wrote several letters denouncing the war. When the letters were printed in Tory newspapers, he fled to England.

Charles Lee (1731–1782) had been a British officer before the Revolution. He settled in Virginia in 1775 and was appointed a major general, second only to Washington. Lee was taken prisoner in December 1776, and during that time, he proposed a plan to British General Howe for winning the war. His betrayal wasn't discovered until almost a century later. After being freed in a prisoner exchange, Lee nearly lost the battle of Monmouth by failing to support Washington at a critical moment. Many suspected he purposely tried to lose the battle so that he could replace Washington as commander in chief. A court-martial found him guilty of "disobedience and misbehavior." He was suspended from the Continental Army for a year, and after writing a vicious letter to the Congress, he was dismissed from service.

Now a British General

Arnold's plot had failed, and Clinton grieved over André's death. Nevertheless, he welcomed Arnold to New York and made him a British brigadier general. Arnold's financial situation improved dramatically. Clinton agreed to pay him 6,000 pounds in addition to a general's pay and a lifetime pension. After her return to Philadelphia, Peggy was banished from Pennsylvania, and she and their three sons eagerly rejoined Arnold in New York.

British General Arnold formed his own Loyalist regiment and called it the American Legion. Late in 1780, he sailed for Virginia with a 1,600-man invasion force. Washington tried to have him kidnapped, but Arnold boarded a ship before Washington could carry out his plan. For the next six months, Arnold stormed through Virginia, destroying supplies, ships, and warehouses. He must have worried about his own safety, however. When he asked a junior officer what might happen to him if he were captured by Patriots, the officer replied, "They will cut off that leg of yours wounded at Quebec and at Saratoga, and bury it with all the honors of war, and then hang the rest of you..."

Victory at Yorktown

Arnold's troublesome raids in Virginia came too late to help the British. The redcoats stationed in the South found themselves constantly under attack by the American Continentals and militia. Washington had sent General Greene south to reorganize the army after the disaster in Camden, South Carolina. Greene and Daniel Morgan, now a general, kept increasing the pressure on the Loyalists and British, under the command of General Charles Cornwallis. The British often won these battles, but Cornwallis found his army so weakened that he retreated into Virginia.

Washington fired the first cannon at the battle of Yorktown in October 1781.

He planned to link up with Arnold's Loyalists, and he counted on the British navy to bring reinforcements from Clinton's men in New York.

In August 1781, Cornwallis took up a defensive position at Yorktown, on the Virginia coast. Far to the north, Washington saw his chance to make a strike with lightning speed, and he took it. Washington raced toward Virginia with both a French army and his own Continental Army. At the same time, a French naval fleet fought a hard battle against the British fleet off the Virginia coast. The British were forced back to New York for repairs, and Cornwallis was trapped at Yorktown.

As a final battle loomed, Arnold left Virginia. He returned to New York and made one more strike against his former country. On September 6, 1781, Arnold landed a raiding party on the Connecticut coast in order to destroy Patriot weapons and supplies. They inflicted heavy damage in New London, not far from his boyhood home. A few weeks later, he and Peggy set sail for England.

The following month, the French and American armies under Washington advanced against Yorktown. After two weeks of heavy bombardment, the British surrendered on October 19, 1781. The Americans had won their independence after more than six years of war.

Chapter 6

SEARCHING FOR STABILITY

$\mathcal{T}$he Arnolds arrived in London in January 1782. At first, they were pleased with the welcome they received. They were invited to the royal court, where Arnold discussed the war with King George III. The queen was captivated by Peggy. The Arnolds settled into what seemed a comfortable London life. They were joined by Arnold's sister, Hannah, and by his three older sons. Although they were only adolescents, Arnold's older sons had been made honorary officers in his American Legion. (It was customary to award the sons of high-ranking officers.)

Four more children were born to Peggy and Benedict. Two of the children died in infancy, a common tragedy in the eighteenth century. The Arnolds still had five sons and a daughter.

The Arnolds Try Canada

Benedict Arnold's life was never comfortable for long. He soon realized that his income was not large enough for the London social whirl. In 1785, he and his family moved to Canada. They chose to live in St. John, a coastal city in the province of New Brunswick, where thousands of Loyalists had moved. Arnold purchased a ship and once again sailed the seas to the West Indies.

Arnold soon had a thriving business. He began buying farmland and town lots, hoping to make a fortune in real estate. But there was little money in Canada, and he found it harder and harder to collect the money people owed him. Many of the Loyalist settlers began to resent the Arnolds' wealth in the midst of so much hardship. They grumbled that Arnold had become rich by selling out his country. When his warehouse and store were destroyed by fire, he could not collect the insurance money because a former partner accused him of having the fire set. By 1792, the Arnolds were ready to return to England.

Creating a Stable Government

Americans were also engaged in a search for stability. The victory at Yorktown ended the Revolution. But now Americans had to decide how power would be distributed between the state and the national governments. The Articles of Confederation had created a central government that was too weak to hold the nation together. The Congress was unable to impose taxes, and therefore could not settle war debts, including the back pay of many Continental soldiers. Each state printed its own currency, and soon these different versions of paper money became worthless.

During the American Revolution, the powerful Iroquois nation and several other tribes fought alongside the British. They were convinced that a British victory offered them the best hope of keeping their tribal lands from land-hungry American settlers. Iroquois warriors, led by the Mohawk chief Joseph Brant, terrorized white settlements throughout New York State. (The Mohawk people belonged to the League of the Iroquois).

After the war, Brant and other leaders of eastern tribes established friendly relations with the new American nation. Several tribes hoped to preserve their lands by adopting the customs of European-based culture. They settled on farms and built towns with schools and churches. During the national Confederation government (1781–1789), Congress urged Americans of European background to use the "utmost good faith" in dealing with Native Americans.

Peaceful relations between white settlers and Native Americans proved to be impossible, though, because of the settlers' constant hunger for more land. In the 1830s, President Andrew Jackson and the Congress began an "Indian Removal Policy," forcing nearly all of the eastern tribes to move west of the Mississippi River. The tribes who were already in the West fared no better. As the American frontier shifted westward throughout the nineteenth century, the western tribes were eventually forced onto government reservations.

Shays' Rebellion

Massachusetts was determined to pay its war debts, and the state demanded that citizens pay their taxes with gold or silver. This was particularly difficult for farmers, who were generally not well off financially. Thousands of farmers who could not pay either lost their farms or went to debtors prison. In the winter of 1786–1787, a veteran named Daniel Shays led an uprising of farmers that became known as "Shays' Rebellion." The rebels tried to seize weapons at an arsenal, but they were quickly scattered by militia. Their rebellion was proof that the nation was in a state of chaos and needed a stronger central authority.

Even before the uprising, a number of Revolutionary leaders, including Washington, had met to discuss ways of strengthening the Confederation government. By the spring of 1787, they persuaded Congress that a convention should be called.

A Constitution Is Written

The Constitutional Convention met in Philadelphia during the summer of 1787. The meeting of 56 delegates brought together some of the most brilliant political thinkers in the nation's history. Over a ten-week period of debate and compromise, the delegates hammered out the Constitution of the United States. The Constitution described the system of government that remains in effect today.

When state conventions were held to ratify the document, many Americans still feared the creation of a strong national government. They were promised that a bill of rights would be added and would become the first ten amendments to the Constitution. Once most Americans were reassured that their liberties would be protected, the Constitution was ratified. The new government went into effect in 1789, and George Washington was elected as the first president.

The Final Years

Arnold spent his last ten years struggling with the same problems that had plagued him throughout his life. He continued his frantic struggle to win more wealth, and he defended his injured sense of honor.

In Great Britain, the Tory party was out of power, after bearing the blame for losing the American colonies. The government was now controlled by the Whigs, who were more sympathetic toward America. As a result, Arnold had few friends in government.

A parade in honor of the federal Constitution, which was ratified by the states in 1788.

In 1792, when a member of Parliament made dark hints about Arnold as a traitor, Arnold challenged the man to a duel. Neither man was hurt, and Arnold had the satisfaction of receiving an apology.

In 1793, the French Revolution led to a new war between Great Britain and France, and Arnold saw another chance to restore his reputation. When he did not receive a general's commission, he armed a ship and entered the war as a privateer (a ship licensed to seize enemy goods). For several years, he was again in the West Indies, where he made, and lost, small fortunes. After he was captured by the French, Arnold managed a daring escape. In 1798, the British government rewarded him for his bravery with a grant of 13,400 acres of land in Canada.

The large plot of land did nothing to improve Arnold's deteriorating finances, though, and Arnold was burdened by other problems. His health was declining: He suffered from pain in both of his legs and had severe asthma, which made it impossible for him to return to sea. In 1796, his oldest son, Benedict, was killed in military action. The loss was devastating to him, and Arnold became withdrawn even from Peggy, who had supported him through all their hardship. By early 1801, he seemed to have lost the will to fight. His health grew steadily worse, and he died on June 14, 1801, at the age of 60. Peggy spent her last years paying off the family's debts. She died of cancer in 1804.

Strange Surprises

In death, there were some strange surprises. When Arnold's will was read, Peggy learned that he had a child in Canada. She dutifully paid the child's mother the amount Arnold requested in his will. When Peggy died, there was another surprise: Among her possessions was a locket (necklace) containing a lock of hair. Women sometimes wore lockets in those days containing the hair of someone they loved. The hair in Peggy's locket belonged to Major John André.

A memorial plaque in Dead River, Maine, honors Arnold's invasion of Quebec.

Benedict Arnold was buried in a small church graveyard. Unfortunately, a careless clerk misspelled his name on the church's burial records. In the late 1800s, the cemetery was moved. Because of the clerk's error, Arnold's tombstone was destroyed. This final act of fate helped to nearly erase all traces of a superb military leader, a daring man who fought valiantly for two countries on opposing sides.

Chronology

The Life of Benedict Arnold

January 14, 1741	Benedict Arnold born in Norwich Town, Connecticut.
1757	French invade New York colony; Arnold joins militia.
1762	Completes apprenticeship; opens apothecary shop.
1767	Marries Margaret Mansfield.
May 10, 1775	Arnold and Ethan Allen lead capture of Fort Ticonderoga.
September 1775	Arnold and General Philip Schuyler launch invasions of Canada
December 1775	American assault on Quebec fails; Montgomery killed, Arnold wounded.
October 1776	Arnold's fleet stalls British on Lake Champlain.
February 1777	Passed over for promotion.
April 1777	Leads heroic fight in Danbury, Connecticut.
August 1777	Leads relief of Fort Stanwix, New York.
September 19 and October 7, 1777	Fights heroically in first and second battles of Saratoga; is wounded in leg.
June 1778	Becomes military governor of Philadelphia.
January 1779	Pennsylvania files charges against Arnold for abuse of power.
April 1779	Marries Peggy Shippen.
Summer–Autumn 1779	Sends military information to the British.
May 1780	Offers to turn West Point over to the British.
August 1780	Takes command of West Point.
September 1780	André is captured by Patriot militia; Arnold's plot is revealed. Arnold flees to New York.
November 1780	Arnold leads his American Legion in invasion of Virginia.
Winter–Summer 1781	Leads destructive raids through Virginia.
December 1781	Sails for England.
1785	Settles in St. John, New Brunswick, Canada for 6 years; then returns to England.

| 1798 | British reward Arnold with land grant in Canada. |
| June 14, 1801 | Benedict Arnold dies in London. |

The Life of the Nation

1756	Seven Years' War begins—a global struggle for empire between Britain and France.
1763	British wins Seven Years' War; expanded empire includes Canada.
1764	Parliament passes Quartering and Currency Acts, angering colonists.
1765	Parliament passes Stamp Act, leading to widespread protests. Stamp Act Congress meets in New York. Daughters of Liberty organize boycotts.
March 1770	British soldiers kill five Boston Patriots at Boston Massacre.
December 16, 1773	At Boston Tea Party, Patriots dump 45 tons of tea into Boston Harbor.
Spring 1774	Parliament passes Coercive Acts.
September 1774	First Continental Congress meets in Philadelphia.
April 19, 1775	Colonial militia fight British at Lexington and Concord
June 1775	Second Continental Congress forms Continental Army, with George Washington as commander.
July 4, 1776	Congress approves Declaration of Independence.
December 1776	Washington's Continental Army wins battle of Trenton.
September–October 1777	British win battle of Brandywine Creek. Howe and British occupy Philadelphia.
October 7, 1777	American victory at second battle of Saratoga is turning point of Revolution.
Winter 1777–78	Continental Army remains at Valley Forge under difficult conditions.
February 1778	French sign alliance with America and declare war on Britain.
December 1778	British seize Savannah, Georgia.
May 1780	5,000 Americans surrender at Charleston, South Carolina; worst American defeat of war.
October 19, 1781	Americans win battle of Yorktown, ending American Revolution.
Winter 1786–87	Shays' Rebellion rocks Massachusetts.
1788	U.S. Constitution ratified. George Washington elected first president.

Glossary

court-martial A military or naval court of law made up of officers; a trial by court-martial.

mercenary A paid soldier.

militia Citizen soldiers with little discipline or training who served in town and state units during the Revolution; they sometimes fought well, but often fled from battles.

Minutemen Militia units ready to fight the British at a moment's notice.

musket A heavy gun carried on the shoulder; less accurate than a rifle.

privateer An armed merchant ship, licensed to attack and capture enemy shipping.

redoubt A sturdy log barricade, often 7 or 8 feet high, with small openings through which defenders could shoot.

Source Notes

Chapter One

Page 6: "I was a coward until I was fifteen." Willard Sterne Randall. *Benedict Arnold: Patriot and Traitor.* New York: William Morrow & Co., 1990, p. 29.

Page 10: "Oh, when shall we be so happy…" James Kinley Martin. *Benedict Arnold: Revolutionary Hero.* New York: New York University Press, 1997, p. 51.

Page 12: "Good God! Are Americans all asleep…" Randall, p. 68

Page 16: "Our friends and neighbors are being mowed down…" Ibid., p. 83.

Page 19: "Never has such a rabble been distinguished…" David C. King. *United States History.* Menlo Park, CA: Addison-Wesley, 1987, p. 83.

Chapter Two

Page 21: "When you consider the badness…" Martin, p. 123.

Page 22: "the shaving soap…lip salve…" George F. Scheer and Hugh F. Rankin. *Rebels and Redcoats: The American Revolution Through the Eyes of Those Who Fought and Lived It.* New York: World Publishing, 1957, p. 120.

Page 22: "when we arose to march…" Ibid.

Page 23: "He was still shouting…" Randall, p. 221.

Page 25: "I have no thought of leaving…" Kenneth Roberts, ed. *March to Quebec: Journal of the Members of the Arnold Expedition.* New York: Doubleday & Doran, 1938, p. 138.

Page 26: "Britain has at last driven America…" King, p. 94.

Page 26: "If we separate from Brtain…" Ibid., p. 108.

Page 28: "remember the ladies…" David C. King. *The United States and Its People.* Menlo Park, CA: Addison-Wesley, 1995, p. 127.

Page 29: "We have in common…" Randall, p. 342.

Page 32: "He is active, judicious…" King. *The United States and Its People*, p. 106.

Chapter Three

Page 36: "[Independence] means no more than this…" Richard Hofstadter, ed. *Great Issues in American History: From the Revolution to the Civil War, 1765–1865.* New York: Vintage Books, 1958, p. 59.

Page 38: "Nothing could exceed the bravery…" Richard Wheeler. *Voices of 1776.* Erie, PA: Meridan Books, 1997, p. 222.

Page 39: "Arnold's intention to quit this department…" Martin, p. 390.

Page 42: "In the same leg…" Kenneth Roberts, ed. *March to Quebec: Journal of the Members of Arnold's Expedition.* New York: Doubleday & Doran, 1938, p. 127.

Page 43: "a day of rejoicing…" Ibid., p. 424.

Chapter Four

Page 45: "for some days past…" L. Edward Purcell and David W. Burg, eds. *World Almanac of the American Revolution.* New York: World Almanac, 1992, p. 161.

Page 47: "We were all in love with her…" Randall, p. 392.

Page 49: "a set of wretches beneath the notice…" Ibid., p. 449.

Page 49: "If your Excellency thinks me criminal…" Ibid., p. 452

Page 50: "imprudent and improper." Ibid., p. 494.

Page 51: "exhibit anew those noble qualities…" Ibid., p. 495.

Page 51: "I may venture to assert…" Purcell and Burg, p. 242.

Chapter Five

Page 54: "To the Inhabitants of America." Randall, p. 575.

Page 54: "Render, brave general…" Ibid., p. 500.

Page 58: "Her sufferings were so eloquent…" Scheer and Rankin, p. 384.

Page 58: "Treason of the blackest dye…" Ibid., p. 384.

Page 58: "for the torrent of blood…" Randall, p. 306.

Page 59: "I pray you to bear me witness…" James Thatcher. *Military Journal of the American Revolution.* Reprinted by *The New York Times* and Arno Press, 1969, p. 272.

Page 60: "They will cut off that leg of yours…" Martin, p. 431.

Further Reading

Benson, John. *The Declaration of Independence with Short Biographies of Its Signers.* Bedford, MA: Applewood Books, 1997.

Carter, Alden R. *The American Revolution: War for Independence* (A First Book). Danbury, CT: Franklin Watts, 1992.

Dolan, Edward F. *The American Revolution: How We Fought the War of Independence.* Brookfield, CT: Millbrook Press, 1995.

King, David C. *America's Story, Book 2: Forming a New Nation.* Littleton, MA: Sundance, 1996.

_____. *The Battle of Saratoga* (Battlefields Across America series). Brookfield, CT: Twenty-First Century Books, 1998.

Purcell, L. Edward, and Burg, David E., eds. *The World Almanac of the American Revolution.* New York: World Almanac, 1992.

Symonds, Craig L. *A Battlefield Atlas of the American Revolution.* Baltimor, MD: Nautical & Aviation Publishing Company of America, 1990.

Web Sites

For more information on the life of Benedict Arnold, go to:
http://www2.interconnect.net/jvera/Jer/Reports/BenedictArnold.html

For information on the events leading up to the American Revolution, including famous people and military battles, go to:
http://users.southeast.net/-dixe/amrev/index.htm

For a chronicle of the American Revolution, as well as photo essays and a game, visit:
http://www.pbs.org/ktca/liberty

For causes, battles, and main events of the Revolution, complete with illustrations, go to:
http://www.multied.com/revolt

To learn more about George Washington, including his role in the American Revolution and his political life, visit:
http://sc94.ameslab.gov/TOUR/gwash.html

For an illustrated history of Fort Ticonderoga, including a timeline, go to:
http://www.neinfo.net/-Fort_Ticonderoga

To learn more about the events leading to the drafting of the Declaration of Independence, go to:
http://lcweb.loc.gov/exhibits/declara/declara2.html

To read the complete Declaration of Independence, visit:
http://www.ecst.csuchico.edu/-rodmur/docs/Declaration.html

Index

BENEDICT ARNOLD AND THE AMERICAN REVOLUTION

post-war government of, 66
    and Seven Years' War, 7–8
    taxation of colonies, 10–11
    and Tea Act, 12
    See also British in North America
Green Mountain Boys, 17–18
Greene, Nathanael, 58, 60

*H*amilton, Alexander, 58
Howe, General William, 25, 30,
    33, 35, 46, 59
Hudson River Valley, 33, 35, 41, 56

*I*ndian Removal Policy, 65
Infant mortality, 63
Intolerable Acts, 14
Iroquois, 34–35, 65

*J*ackson, Andrew, 65
Jameson, James, 56–57
Jefferson, Thomas, 26

*K*nox, Henry, 19, 25
Kosciuszko, Colonel Thaddeus, 38

*L*ake Champlain, battle on,
    30–31
Lathrop, Daniel, 7, 9
Lee, Charles, 59
Lexington, battle of, 15
Livingston, Henry Brockholst, 39
Loyalists, 28–29, 35, 47, 60,
    62, 64
    Arnold and, 46, 54

Canadian, 33, 40
    in South, 46, 51

*M*aine, Arnold's expedition in,
    20–23
Massachusetts
    and war debts, 65
    See also Boston Massacre
McCrea, Jane, 36
Militia, 14
    at Lexington, 15
    and Shays' Rebellion, 65
    in South, 60
    Washington and, 19
    See also Benedict Arnold
Minutemen, 14–15
Mohawks, 65
    Sons of Liberty as, 13–14
Montgomery, General Richard,
    22–24
Morgan, Daniel, 21, 23, 25, 37,
    40–42
Morgan's Rifles, 21, 37–40
Morristown, New Jersey, 30

*N*ative Americans
    and Americans, 35
    and British, 33–36, 39, 65
    and French, 7
    and United States, 65
New France. *See* Canada
New Haven, Connecticut, 8–9,
    12, 14, 16
New Jersey, 30

New London, Connecticut, 62
New York City, 25, 30
    British in, 35, 46
Norwich Town, Connecticut, 6, 59

*P*aine, Thomas, 36
Parliament of Great Britain,
    10–11, 14, 67
Patriots, 11
    and Arnold, 46
    grievances against British, 12, 26
    number of, 28
    preparations for war, 18–19
    propaganda by, 36–37
    strategy of, 16, 18
    See also Americans
Philadelphia, 43, 59
    Arnold in, 46–47, 49
    capture of, 35
    recapture of, 46
Profiteering, 47
Propaganda, 36

*Q*uartering Act, 10
Quebec, Canada, 20, 23–25

*R*edcoats, 18
    See also British
Redoubts, 39
Regulars, 34
Revere, Paul, 36–37

*S*t. John, Canada, 64
St. Leger, Colonel Barry, 34–35

Photo Credits

Pages 15, 28, and 45: Courtesy of The Library of Congress; pages 22 and 41: ©Blackbirch Press; page 37: Courtesy of The New York Public Library, Aster, Lenox and Tilden Foundation; all other illustrations, including cover: North Wind Picture Archives.